OCTOPUSES

Darla Duhaime

Rourke
Educational Media

rourkeeducationalmedia.com

Before & After Reading Activities

Teaching Focus:

Concepts of Print- Have students find capital letters and punctuation in a sentence. Ask students to explain the purpose for using them in a sentence.

Before Reading:

Building Academic Vocabulary and Background Knowledge

Before reading a book, it is important to set the stage for your child or student by using pre-reading strategies. This will help them develop their vocabulary, increase their reading comprehension, and make connections across the curriculum.

1. *Read the title and look at the cover. Let's make predictions about what this book will be about.*
2. *Take a picture walk by talking about the pictures/photographs in the book. Implant the vocabulary as you take the picture walk. Be sure to talk about the text features such as headings, Table of Contents, glossary, bolded words, captions, charts/diagrams, or Index.*
3. Have students read the first page of text with you then have students read the remaining text.
4. *Strategy Talk – use to assist students while reading.*
   - *Get your mouth ready*
   - *Look at the picture*
   - *Think…does it make sense*
   - *Think…does it look right*
   - *Think…does it sound right*
   - *Chunk it – by looking for a part you know*
5. *Read it again.*

Content Area Vocabulary
Use glossary words in a sentence.

burrows
limbs
mollusks
predators

After Reading:

Comprehension and Extension Activity

After reading the book, work on the following questions with your child or students in order to check their level of reading comprehension and content mastery.

1. *Where do octopuses live? (Summarize)*
2. *What do octopuses eat? (Asking Questions)*
3. *How are octopuses like people? (Text to Self Connection)*
4. *How do octopuses escape predators? (Asking Questions)*

Extension Activity

Draw an octopus face on a paper plate. Cut eight limbs from construction paper. Glue the limbs to the plate. Glue a Popsicle stick to the back of the plate. Put on an octopus puppet show!

Table of Contents

Amazing Octopuses

A octopus has no bones. Its body is mostly muscle. Its organs are protected inside its thick mantle.

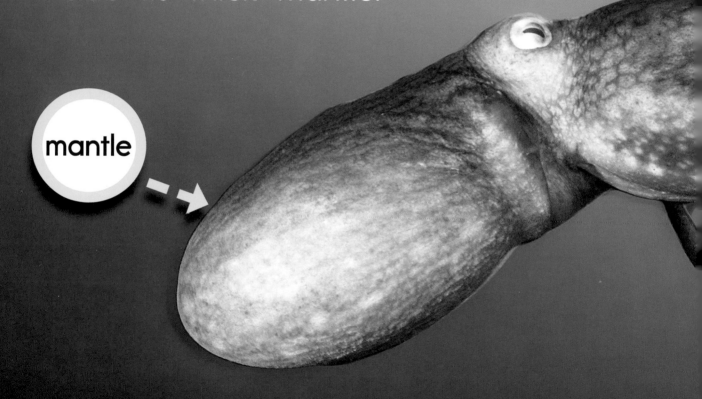

mantle

The mantle is surrounded by eight **limbs**. The limbs are lined with suction cups.

suction cups

Two of the limbs act like legs. They help the octopus walk on the seafloor.

An octopus has a beak. Its beak crushes the crabs, lobsters, and **mollusks** an octopus eats.

beak

Under the Sea

Octopuses live alone. They dig **burrows** or make dens in rocks or coral.

14

Sharks, dolphins, and eels eat octopuses. An octopus may hide in a shell to avoid these **predators**.

If an octopus feels threatened, it releases ink. The ink darkens the water. Then the octopus swims away!

ink

Smart and Colorful

An octopus can change color. They can match their surroundings. They may also change color to scare predators!

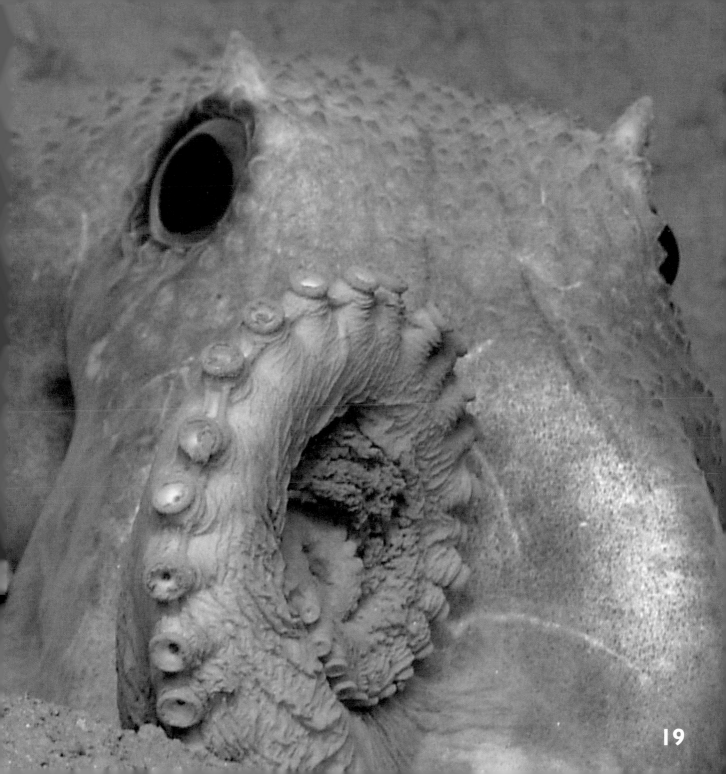

19

Octopuses are smart. They can navigate mazes, solve problems quickly, and play!

Fun Facts

🐙 An octopus has three hearts! One pumps blood to its organs. The others pump blood to its gills.

🐙 Octopuses have blue blood.

🐙 An octopus's suction cups can sense taste.

🐙 A 50-pound (23-kilogram) octopus can squeeze through a hole that is only two inches (five centimeters) wide!

Picture Glossary

 **burrows** (BUR-ohs): Tunnels or holes in the ground used as a home by an animal.

 **limbs** (limz): Parts of a body used for moving or grasping.

 **mollusks** (MAH-luhsks): Animals with soft bodies, no spine, and hard shells that live in water.

 **predators** (PRED-uh-turs): Animals that hunt other animals for food.

23

Index

Websites to Visit

http://kids.nationalgeographic.com/animals/octopus/#octopus.jpg

www.sciencekids.co.nz/sciencefacts/animals/octopus.html

www.softschools.com/facts/animals/octopus_facts/23

Meet The Author!
www.meetREMauthors.com

About the Author

Darla Duhaime is fascinated by sea creatures and their amazing ocean habitats. When she is not writing books for kids, you can often find her gazing at the ocean, dreaming up new stories.

www.rourkeeducationalmedia.com

PHOTO CREDITS: Cover

Edited by: Keli Sipperley
Cover and Interior design by: Rhea Magaro-Wallace

Library of Congress PCN Data

Octopuses / Darla Duhaime
(Ocean Animals)
ISBN (hard cover)(alk. paper) 978-1-68342-327-0
ISBN (soft cover) 978-1-68342-423-9
ISBN (e-Book) 978-1-68342-493-2
Library of Congress Control Number: 2017931174

Printed in the United States of America, North Mankato, Minnesota